Wolf Laundry

Lisa Creech Bledsoe

More poetry, wildflowers, and mountain at
AppalachianGround.com

Praise for *Appalachian Ground*

"Author Lisa Creech Bledsoe brings together the natural world of the Appalachian mountains, autobiography and life lessons in a book rich in imagery and wisdom. From meditations to help empty your mind to simple appreciation of the color brown, from lessons learned as a beekeeper and theologian, Bledsoe's words are a gift in an age where we don't stop to look at wildflowers near enough, where beauty has faded to gray in stress-filled times. I am looking forward to her next volume. In the meantime, I will read a poem each night as a lullaby and meditation." —Sis Steele

"*Appalachian Ground* by Lisa Creech Bledsoe hit my mailbox today. I started reading and am one step short of levitating in wonder and joy. The poet and I have been friends for decades. Because of that (or even so), reading her work I feel as though a shooting star befriended me all those years ago and it/she and I have been falling falling falling — oxygen: yes; gravity: no — together forever." —Mary Jo Cartledgehayes

"*Appalachian Ground* paints word pictures that stir my soul and bring forth pictures of the good Earth and its abundance. Lisa has a way with words that evokes wonderful images and touches the heart. Thank you for the great book and its way of offering a calm look at the world and our existence." — Greg Lundberg

"This book is a tribute to all things Appalachian. Don't miss taking this mountain adventure with the author. She takes you along with her and the animals through the woods on simple adventures that turn into much, much more. Very enjoyable and heartwarming." —K.M.R.

"Shades of Mary Oliver, Rumi, Emerson, Hemingway and Rilke echo through the sacred hills and valleys of Bledsoe's writing. Some lines hit with the punch of a bare-knuckled boxer, others dance softly like a mountain stream in autumn. Lisa writes from a depth of hard-carved experience, sketching open the very corners of human existence with her words. Read her words and let the mountains call you home to yourself. You won't regret it." —Titanium

"She loves her mountain, and it loves her back, bringing beauty and wisdom to her to put down in words. But without an open heart and mind, and an eye to see beauty, and the right words in the right order, all the mountain's gifts would have gone for naught. But they have not. Read these poems, and weep for the hope to see and hear as Lisa Creech Bledsoe sees and hears. And be grateful that she has shared her world with us." —J. Blackburn

Table of Contents

I. Wild Woman Chair

Three Breaths

What would it take for you—
just for a moment—
to feel light and unburdened

The thinnest communion wafer
held before the window
atoms shimmering

eager to burst apart and ascend but
held together by quantum threads
gushing light

Once you become buoyant
you can watch the blue
weights plummet earthward

The unsubstantial will lift away
and take you with it
    What would it take for you—

just for a moment—three breaths?
to step into the tideway
of energy and life

Render your burdens unto the earth
they are not yours after all
but the center of the silver sky

three breaths will give you clear
humming wings and leave the taste
of flowers on your lips

Mandala to Please the Crow

You are forever asking for a story

Instead I will tell you
how velvety your black wings
look under the winter sun

Instead I will sit
in the wild woman chair
and tell you that the moss maidens
dream of wings
baptized with water
bathed in frost
absolved by sky

Instead I give you mandala
a laughing mountain song
in appreciation of the way
we are sealed with clay
to one another's stories

Crow Poem-Song

For the weed-woman
who talks to the moss:

Your stories are good
about us and we watch
linger-drifting
you gather and share
temple of pebble, string and seed

Of course they love us—
the moss maidens, weed-woman
yellow yellow leaf-flutter
tangle dreaming

We are puzzle-wise
preening winter blue-glint wings
calling in the glitter frost

Send our caw-gift them
water icy water gift
saturate rinse restore
stems spores filaments
ruffle shake tremble shiver
winter water blessing to the
ancient green-wise elders
and their offspring

Make more song-stories
caw-gift stronger
rising on the thermals
from the wild woman chair

Fire Pink

In the garden where the wild beasts were kept
you had your genesis

One birth, one theft, many deceptions
but miracles also
seeping out slowly over the years
never quite keeping ahead of the damage
but still, bread from angels

It was important to him that you be
lovely to look at, and you were
but not for the reasons he believed

Always you were the fox, ahead of the wolf
the cat, ahead of the fox,
the crow, ahead of the cat

You are clever with a skin and feather
having sewn, spun, and
redeemed them, coins from
six thousand empties gathered on the highway
for yourself and others

Always you were the bail, ahead of the bondsman
the check, ahead of the repo man
yoga breathing to stave off panic
gitchee and boogey

Your survival knife is a deadly
trick blade, a razored cipher —
you are still learning the passwords and enigmas

Even so, it keeps you out of court
until the system can be overturned
the tower razed
wounds exposed to the sun

Until then, they think you are the flower
but in truth
you are the unchained breath of flame,
the roots that break stone and beast

You leave behind only
the scent of smoke, cloves
and the psalm of a shining river

What the Owl Doesn't Know

Today again I searched the woods
craning my neck, straining
to see the dark humped
slump of rags
and dapple

I scoured the leaf litter
beneath the great pines
oak and bitternut
for pellets filled
with fur and bones

In daylight he is the exact shape of a miss
a black pit in the white
oiled bowl of noon

In the dark he studies ambush
ten strikes for two kills
the wreckage of mouse, sod and thorn

All that, no one disrespects

But there are limits still
and mysteries he's never heard

Bees are one secret
the owl doesn't know

He has never heard
the hives winging up
like a symphony
released to the sun

Doesn't know the blackberry's sticky kiss
the furzling of morning glories
or the refreshment of wet seep and sand
under a blazing day

The owl is mute
on the subject of maps written
in pulse and vibration
or the pleasure of maths
and ancient honeycraft

And should we ever meet
under the shadows
as I hope

I will not tell him

In the Beginning

In the beginning, there was possibility.
Everywhere there was the open, the waiting, the
imaginable.

A sigh of promise flowed
along the throat of the open,
and grew luminous with love.

That which glowed soon shone.
That which shone soon blazed with energy and joy:
the light of love sang into life.

This shining love was not separate from the beginning;
it was the beginning.
It was the hymn and heartbeat of all.

The lovesong grew stronger as it played.
It surged and expanded, and soon bright patterns began
to weave themselves within the song.

And so the skies and waters were born,
and the many lands and lights and creatures.
These were not separate from the lovesong,
they were the lovesong,
and the more they played,
the more new refrains and choruses arose,
all filled with the love and light from which they came.

We are not separate from the love,
the light, or the song.
We are not separate from the skies and waters,
the lands and lights, or from any of the creatures.

We are in them, and they are in us.
Together we are the hymn and heartbeat of all.

Still Life

Walk on the mountain, and don't hurry.

Inhabit the poetry of being.
Attend.
Pause.
Plenty of white space at the end of each step.

Today, a cat resting in the leaves.
An earthstar near the end of snowmelt.
Seven hollow snail shells, and
a woollybear at the gate of dreams.

As Day Leaves

the mud puts away her mischief
ferns and feverfew hush the wind to stillness
shagbarks fold in
their wrens
and phoebes

white
winks the moon

as day leaves
the warren nestles her clutch of hares
swallowtails and fritillaries are soothed
with milkweed and
whisper-grasses

evening primrose
glows
while roots
drowse
in their beds

the bees
huzzle together
as day leaves

and just

as she
tiptoes
out

and

turns

the key

to shhhut

the

woods

the owl's alarm goes off

Crawfish

There is a clever brown crawfish who lives in our spring.

She has an adroitness I envy; a balance I seek. She
walks forward but swims backward—she is both
yielding and fierce. She has no bones, but constructs her
armor from the mineral-rich water in which she lives.
Her children will not be born until she deems it time,
until the sun has given her all the warmth she desires.
These are just a few of her mysteries.

How often and loudly the world scolds us to stop hiding,
to move always ahead. But when I slowly unright the
the rocks beneath the rills, I must look behind where I
think the crawfish might be. This is how she tricks the
heron with his sharp beak; she moves according to her
own needs.

Shall we build our strength from soft things? From the
water, a muddy bank, and the willingness to sit quietly,
hidden in the woods by the spring? Shall we compel the
devotion of the sun?

If I am quick to learn her tricky ways, I might hold her
a moment, before she leaps backward into the water—
laughing, and leaving me small pink pinch marks to
remember her with.

Story by Story

Story by story I am being forged.

My son carries throwing knives on his hip,
a small packet of restlessness tucked behind his heart.

A black bear opened our birdfeeder
like an origami flower and galloped
away at the clang of a pot lid.

In this poem there are a goldfinch,
a tangle of new-hatched snakes with yellow necklaces,
and lunch tied in a bandanna.

The songs that daily raise the house of my devotion
send me again to inspect his progress on the treehouse
in the long green woods,
to name the new wildflower in the field or
find the ridge above the rhododendrons.

I have a knife, a hand-drawn map,
cool water from the well.

We eat our apples and boiled eggs on a
hidden bench in the meadow
bathed in every hue
and lingering note of glory.

Henry, Returned

An empty field in winter
snow bowing the electric fence lines

Henry, king of cats, reigns
in this field —
which he never knew in life —
irritable as ever, but
unperturbed to find himself returned
in my poem
in my snow-blue field

The shadows flicker with his small dark princess —
the one who filled his heart only to break it
when she left him, at the end of her years

Big old Henry watches a coyote trot across the ridge
and I stand here a while longer
as the snow mounts

The World Reflected in a Scarlet Elf Cup

Chilly morning rain
trees drinking their cup of sky
me, bundled and
upside down
peering into the Everything

The Librarian of Spring

When the robin alights on the brown thatch
of last year's grass, I stop scraping mud
and leaf litter from my boots and listen.

The pines cease their whispering and stand straighter;
the cat at the edge of the wood comes quivering
to attention.

The robin pins us all with his glossy black eye
saying without speaking: There is work to be done.

He is the implacable librarian of spring
briskly ordering the season,
unerringly plucking soft or chitinous pleasures
from the leaf-lined season's shelves.

Open his breast and you will find a fire ablaze
in a clean stone hearth, and tall windows
flung open to the sun.
Wisdom lights the center of every cell.

All that must be done, will be done.

Tea as Winter Ends

She tracks in mud and moss
and sets about heating water
for tea

This is the sound of miracles

II. Red Velvet Couch

Now Gathered

What is rolling toward us
in great coils, unspooling
cascades over you and me and the cats
walking together down the dappled drive

I have spoken my desires into a cup
and poured it into the offering pool:
Look what has come!
To hold it you must give up planning and worry
even wisdom, release a thousand
years ago and tomorrow
in the name of all love
which today is splendor arriving with every step

This is the sanctuary of now
this quiet road, these cows and crows
and locust trees, heavy with cream blooms
heady with now-ness, replete with gift

I am subsumed by *at once*
we are full of *this moment:*
I reach up for *right away*
and the flowers flood down into my basket
leaving my hands sticky with nectar

Looking back from the locust tree to the shadows
where you are keeping the cats from the road
your smile is a bolt of light
your presence a secret meadow
I want to rush in, again
plunge in and drink the deep
green cave of you

And I do, still *now*
still in the sanctuary
which sings and claps and rolls with us
reverberating with the thunder of delight
back up the dappled drive, the mountain
with cats running zig-zag ahead—
so much resonant, irreproachable *now*

We return to our soft house
folded of brown velvet, stitched with silver
to share a meal, a cup
drifted with sweet locust blooms
then lay ourselves down side by side
for an afternoon nap
under the satisfied gaze of today

Alphabet of the Heart

For Lauren

As it happened
I was both charmed and annoyed—

mostly annoyed because
alphabetically in my heart's dictionary
annoyed was in it's proper place

but after a nap, a walk in the woods
and a second look at the ridiculous situation

I moved charmed up to its place
at the front

Both words belong, of course

If not for annoying
none of us would have a baby sister—

and if not for charmed
we'd never notice her beautiful, messy curls
or impish grin

Both together are what make you
trade her a piece of your
grown-up big sister spearmint gum
and get in return one of
the fruity flavor she chose—

which you like so much better
but were pretending was babyfied

At Nineteen

He invited a new friend over
and cooked us all breakfast.
I can't remember when he last did this.

She was beautiful, of course.
They are.

She washed the dishes
and left a cluster of new pennies
on the windowsill, winking in the sun.

Cloudmade

For Lindsay and Harper

the dream pulled you down
held you by your untraveled
longing, rocked you
in the lap of the woods
until you became
a woman who discovered
clouds (which—
were there all along)
a promise of rain, an anthem
and you sunk down
deep fibers in the measure
of her small shape, luminous
biding

I remember saving honey
from our hives for you
and watching you tell
me, when we finally
were together,
that she would come—
how your face shone!

now you will be
blessed with rainfall, with
hoarfrost and the grinning
soul of the sun herself,
hailshock and tornado—
all of it, which you will
receive
standing in front of your
cloud-mirror saying,

I am a mother
I am a mother

the hive murmurs assent
the sea is glass and love, you feel
electricity, message
and music running root to root
in the grove of your dream
under the storm

Cafe Love Poem

a glossy white plate
eight small rolls of crab, rice, nori
pale gold ginger in graceful folds
ahhh wasabi

the puddles are still roofed with ice
but light blazes through the cafe
and my eyes water
with the intolerable brightness of love

Avocado Love Poem

I love you with
these sweet white onions
stinging our noses
and lemon juice
slipping down my wrist

I love you with poblanos
tasting of the earth,
peppery serranos and garlic
to heal and make us strong

We are two succulent green halves;
my heart is cupped in your bowl
with the scarlet glaze—
your mouth makes my skin pebble

I will marry you again
and carry a bouquet of cilantro

Night Flight

The closet light hums and flickers
but refuses me.
Shivering, I see your empty shoes
slender and neat in the shadows.

Remember that day in Umstead–
the missed trailheads and unplanned miles—

The tiny dark grotto below the spillway
where we unlaced our boots,
peeled our sweaty socks inside out
and settled on the stones
to cool our feet in the black water—

We talked and watched for snakes.

When I felt the first tiny sting, I started!
And a dozen bright minnows scattered
like a fistful of thrown dimes.

Remember the crackers from our packs—
how we coaxed back our silvery hosts?

What use are maps?

We watch for snakes
but trust our soft feet to the trails
boots, and minnows.

Your flight arrives tonight.

Traveling Back

don't tell me please
this is all you will walk
you were up all night
and we have come to the end
of the field, drenched
with morning

there are fields yet and
white wood anemones to surprise us
in the pine shadows
where the trail hides from the sun

you never tire before me
although
you do have more sense
when it comes to halfway points
and the gravity of traveling back

I know you thought by now
to be ensconced in book shelves
traffic noises and
ordinary black umbrellas,
a library within walking distance

but

you have also loved
a boot scraper by the porch
the heady pleasure of honey in July
crawdads and blue creeks
and me, turning stones

perhaps with grace
I will bow to your practical heart
your steady thrum
and tomorrow or the day after
we will walk endlessly
together in the yellow fields

Take and Drink

To my 16 year old son

There's nothing but water in the holy pools—
the brown ponds where cows wade
the baptismal fonts and
rivers filled with speckled trout.

You should run your fingers through it
dot it on your head and breast and shoulders
splash it toward your young girlfriend
and laugh loudly together.

Dip both hands wholly in and
rub your palms together, then
slide your burning fingers
up the insides of her arms.

Scoop it up, wash your face,
let it sluice down and mold your shirt to your chest.

Slick back her hair with poured handfuls
and let the rest spill blessing into both your mouths.

Take and drink, drink and be filled.

Without Words

In the auditorium of the earth
the elephant speaks with urgency
dark phonemes, flowing consonants
that pulsate along the folds between worlds
and emerge with knowledge at the feet
of her daughter, miles away

In the syllabary of the hive
the sacred songs are unwritten but known
in charged shiverings
math and scented consonance
the disclosures of a thousand atomic drums

Stop looking and
let the language confide in your skin
suffuse your neural circuits
report to the family of your bones

Sit in the kitchen and feel your way

More is shared in
the shuffling beneath the table
the scraping of cup and bench
than is spoken

For Greg

At the lake today, scattering grackles
and last season's sweet gum balls from the trail
I think of you.

You used to live just over there
across the silver water.
I once spelled my name in forks on
your kitchen counter.

The day we met
you charmed me with your disregard for social graces.

And remember when you brought Anne to meet us all
and we sat in the pub, waving smoke from our faces
and toasting the future with vodka tonics, or whisky?
I knew she was the one for you.

You used to live just over there,
past the field with the faded blue truck
and the copper-colored barn;
you know the one.

The air is filled with the smell of wild onions.
I turn my face to let the sun fill up my eyes.

Lunar Eclipse, 1982
For Dick Hooton

alone, eight (and another now)
eight thousand feet above a black ocean
miles from Mineral King
fed by snowmelt and silver
onboard mountain lights

billowing youth, and sailing up
climbing up nightfall
in red fir and jeffrey pine
cloud by cloud, cirrus and cirrostratus

pupils dilating like clocks, like dark shells
deep tides, like gaping mouths
of anglerfish and whale sharks

how untried we were
when the moon slipped
into the well of the earth's shadow
swell, falling, waved

the extraordinary and possible
the subject matter, death
          or life: how
isolated are we, truly?
And how deeply do we accept
the heartbeat and intent of leaping stars?

Whisky Rose

The physics of love is not what we expected.
Our hearts slip along their parabolas, disappear,
then emerge in wildly unforeseen places.
Our fears and addictions take uncanny shapes
in the quantum foam.
There are strange geometries at work here.
We do not navigate them with ease
even after all these years.

A rose the color of fresh peaches
in a green whisky bottle is so much simpler.

Red Velvet Couch

My neighbor
has loaded a tattered
red velvet couch
onto his flatbed truck
and parked it
in the narrow strip of weeds
between his chicken hut
and the river.

There are at least
three poems
in whatever happens next.

Homesick

Today the sunrise startled me.

In the parking lot it was only violet
with the sodium lights crackling
and the school bus.

But then I turned—

And there was pink and pink and
lavender and even green, burning upwards.

But now there is ice and gray
and I ache for the mountains to greet me
with a palm to each of my cheeks
and their mossy breath.

Still Life with Light

An apron's worth of buckeyes gathered—
this afternoon's rain brought them down—
are glistening in crooked rows on the sill.

I steadily fill a yellow bowl with sliced peaches,
lemon juice, and sugar
and set the tea to steep for tomorrow.

The boys will all arrive quite late I think.

I've baked, and laid out fresh linens
which the cats have already found.

The computer glows against your glasses
as you pay bills at the kitchen table;
you sing quietly with Tom Petty about
a lover you've never had.

My breath expands and shakes itself like a coat.

This house gleams against the evening—
there are so many stars.

III. Wolf Laundry

Nestlings

I have put five flecked stones in the offering place
tied five blessing sticks in the yellow birch
where you tried your best
for your hatchlings, but exited young boys
are a flash flood and
the throttle of their go-cart was stuck on high
and spewing smoke

Watching you wing away filled me with heaviness
I got there as quickly as I could
and had them nestled in my shirt
trembling and exhausted

But sometimes rescue isn't enough
the equation is altered, nothing balances any more
a new map has begun
and no one wants to follow the trail

I left an eggshell from the wren's nest
and a sprig of cranesbill by the spring
where the stone below has been smoothed into a bowl
to hold water

The cardboard box with an old dishtowel
and five dying chicks
I carried to a neighbor
and she will do her best, but

The math is all wrong
the weight of grief is too dense
to represent something winged away, leaving us less

This month she would have graduated from high school
and almost certainly would have
made a garden
discovered a gift for chemistry, or a favorite author
and seen some of the gaping cracks in the world,
the peeling sheetrock

I dropped a pinch of salt in the carved spring bowl
for the scraps of breath and words, non-sequiturs
and the wracked anniversaries of our hearts

There is no consolation
in the circle which includes death:
        It matters.
It has consequences which cannot be reversed

And there is a gleam of wise hope
which can sometimes be seen flickering
over the field at night, particularly
against the murky woods where darkness holds fast

You already know
everything will not turn out well

Make gardens anyway—
who knows what will grow there
or who will harvest them

May you be open to holy surprise

My eyes are closed but
I can still see the fireflies, flashing

Salt

In the deep stretch of night
In the stretch of night that nothing can fill
though everything tries:
    a spilled moon
    the hissing snow
    your helpless revolutions of grief

The smallest shift begins
ions relocate
something mineralizes

Despair and movement arise from the same place
Things which have been separated
thirst to be healed

A woman opens her cabinet, brings out a salt cellar
A man starts a journey to the sea
Bees steward these passageways
generations and oceans apart
There are white sutures where the edges meet

It can't be seen
but in front of your door
in front of the part of you
where the firewood
was stacked but now is gone
the snow is turning to slush

Not yet, but soon
a tomato might grow
clean and bright
in that empty pot by the door

Wolf Laundry

I didn't notice anything the first time
the wolf did my laundry

Maybe a faint smell of mouse
and a door ajar somewhere I
wasn't expecting

It wasn't long before
there was an issue with snow drifting in
and gaping boxes in the hallway

I put two white deer bones by the spring
and eighty-sixed dishes because there weren't
any clean

Wasps filled the stove with needles and argument
anyway, and now my dog is gone,
the mail gnawed and stained under the car
where the skunk left it
in feral disrepair

I pull winter onions and tear pine cones
with skinned hands
lamenting all things tender

A neighbor's barn has slipped from its foundation
into icy weeds, inarticulate

Forest flickers and swallows
one meal from wild

Refuge (Spearfinger)

1.
Once upon a time
hïlahi'yu, as the Cherokee say
long, long ago
there was a very hungry woman
or a very angry woman

And it might have been a man

This woman was filled with basalt
night and wasps
the heaviest fevers
of grief

Hardened
with the grim compaction
that holds up oceans,
conceives and births terrible storms

Caustic ash filled her eyes and
clotted in the corners of her mouth

With one long stone-bone finger she speared out
the liver of someone you knew
and devoured it
to assuage her pain

This never worked
but it was what she could think of,
motions her unbending skin would tolerate
and a thousand years later
it was mindless

It was heartless
as the only place she had left
to shelter life
was also the hand of her spear finger

Where her heart clung redly
ever making itself smaller
so as not to be lost entirely

So angry-hungry
Heart-in-hand
Stone-bone woman

2.
What is the refuge of the fugitive
and the hunter?

Have you a place
where both fear and love can be welcomed
and might find rest?

When you walk through the low places,
the weeping places from a thousand years ago
you must bless them
again and again

When you gather stones together
with lichen, seeds, and
other small
great gifts of the mountain's heart
you must bless them
again and again

Bless the caves and shallows in which to crouch
and be sheltered from the hammer of
fear-wind, from the night wolves

Bless the fear, night, and wolves also

3.
May you draw water from the watering place
find food in the offering place, and
refuge in the covering palm of the mountain

May everything within you
be blessed
again and again

With profound gratitude for the Cherokee legend of U`tlun'ta, or Spearfinger

Alchemy

I'm sure you've noticed
the skeletons on the
floor of your unfurnished margins

They get up, link-blink

and amble freely
airing their enigmas
shaking their sly puzzles, phalanges
moldering old ciphers

They get up, up, clatter-tatters

demanding a place
at the table and further
to eat from your golden plate

late

This is not
the true love you envisioned
back when you were a charmed
and furious young woman

but

here they are, unshakable
love-shrunk but
held together by someone else's
iron bands

bumping into you in the hallway and
leaving gruesome bruises
that sometimes break and weep

I've noticed that
sometimes, even
you sleep with them

But isn't it true
don't you think
they seem thinner now
more permeable somehow and
less telling

What would happen
do you think
if you were to groom them a bit
give them a shine and polish
make a better place than
your naked, unheated room
for them to settle, sift

a rosewood cabinet
a satin scarf
the gift of forty winks and
even welcome, find

Unbind them

and you might be changed

Pilgrimage

when you feel you cannot forgive
speak the words anyway, each day
        like petals dropped onto a pond

in your sanctuary of possibility
may your heart say:

I do the daily work of love
and it is good
to circle the holy place
        before entering

Reclamation

Of course you will go out, go out
to rise sing rove among wild ramps
bloodroot staining your heels
the scent of crushed mint and garlic
strong divine

Remember as you increase in wild
even in your refuge
there will be thefts
of pith wool soul

Dance silver-skinned, yes dance
elbow fist spine and
keep a shrewd eye
on your pelt

use your claws to pin it down
stretch it amid thorny canes
smeared with mud from the slough
and stinging nettle

wear many skins fur feathers
whose eyes will watch for you and warn

The world may be lonely for
your milk and hips, your arms
but refuse to be fleeced

though when you have
there will come times to say goodbye
to your children marrow seven
to steal away the key, steal away

what won't be given if you only plead
was yours all along
and go out to the fierce
unbroken
to become yourself again

Healing of the Nations

The dead company you keep
matters the same
as the living

your ancestors are
limned in green and grown
too bright, nearly
to see

but they are there, just
under the trees—
and I know this will puzzle you—
of life

the thousand thousand trees
wreathed between worlds
with promises
tied in their boughs and cradles

bending down their birds
to reach you
with messages
missives, children
ordinary and holy

many of us visit
though
the pass, persuasion
is extraordinarily
convoluted
or at least
conventional travel

is less helpful
in such a place
and requires a certain

credence
and attenuation

don't worry if you miss, lose
your way
it happens all the time

the deep lost
the deep found, foliate, fruit
the forever green
reaches out
to embrace travelers
no less here than there

and

you might be astonished to discover
exactly what you dared not dream
to hope for

there

by the well
beneath the branches

Slow Medicine

Today we unstrung the old electric fence
gathered stones in piles
and leveled a second place on the mountain
above the two stained, empty benches
making a place for a new generation to try

The ragwort has just started to bloom
the bee yard is quiet and
it will snow tomorrow

This time, seven hives wait

We've lost five of five
he lost fourteen of fourteen
they lost nine of ten

Climate change, pesticides
separation, breakdown
the economics of scarcity
next year even more will die

and some will give up
maybe I will, too
seven new hives
his fourteen, their nine
too little, too late

But what if the medicine
is in our slowness

Our foolish refusal to give up
the more beautiful world

both here and not yet
despite fear, grief, more bad news

Can you dedicate yourself
to generational change
to something you'll never live to see?

Can you gaze resolutely toward hope
love deeply the ones who
cannot yet accept love?

Can you give yourself
to slow medicine?

Rest your head and hands
and feet on the earth
give all the gifts you can
to the people and place you've
chosen to love

With every step I
smell the mountain mint, crushed
and rising

Tending the Night Mare

Caught in the bare frost between stars
fear paces and bolts the raw unsheltered
seat and soul, alone

Yesterday a woman wondered:
where does the stream begin?

She pressed her ear to the sodden field
        —listened, knees darkening with wet
and heard a rosy gurgle rise
spiral over whorl and spiral
below the snow-broken weeds

Yesterday the water wondered:
where does the woman begin?

Lavish your fearful gray with
murmuring compassion, rising
spiral over whorl and spiral

Plant her heart with forage and
a song to follow under the ground, then
together well up to the sun
of the mountain's satisfaction

She longs for someone hope-filled
to lead her unbroken into
good fields and stories

May it be you, may it be us

We are, seat and soul, never alone

Traveling Charms

I. What I found when we moved in

a miniature hand-carved dollhouse chair,
eighty-four spent shotgun cartridges by the shed and
nearly as many golf balls in the woods

a cherry dropleaf dining room table, abandoned
eleven mouse skeletons in varying states of decay
on upper closet shelves

an antique cut-glass jelly dish
no larger than my palm
a broken green bathtub and matching toilet
in the yard, and
four wheeled office chairs, circa 1975
in the field of goldenrod and poison ivy
a steep hike above the house

one mattress below the cliff face, twin size,
and the rubbed-smooth soles of two children's shoes
in the creek

II. When you must go

when you have a long journey to make
and there are no songs to memory the way
rise up, say a blessing, and walk
into the open field

tell the bees your story
and the wild garlic or milkweed

for no rite is complete unless it is witnessed
and the open field is a good place to work a charm

remember to use the ancient words:
love, we, ashes, black, flow, mother

begin before light breaks, for trees mutter in their sleep
and secret wisdom may be had for the listening
if they do not feel your weight on their roots,
your small hands on their bark

like the butterflies you
will make the pilgrimage home again
before your reserves are gone
gathering signals in the night then
beginning with the sound of a waterfall

Sounding

Breaths, dishes washed, books started
and set aside —
measures of the deeps of night

Lichens grow one millimeter each year
and live a thousand years, maybe more

So you breathe and start books
then set them aside

You cast a line to sound the fathoms
gauging the depth, hauling in wet rope
hand over hand, rechecking
until morning steps out
against the shrouds
to call in the night

When hail is small it's called an embryo
and is blown high in the storm to freeze and grow

The size of the hail depends
on the power of the wind to keep it aloft
until it is heavy enough to be born

At night the gate of winds
is open or shut, banging
the way clear or clouded

A new future pulls on an oilskin coat
and looks out to see whether or not
it is heavy enough to be born

You can always start again
let the wind bear you high in the wind
to be shaped this time
by a new storm

Three Cups

Alone in the house
breathing the wood-tide damp
washing in the door, left ajar
cool-tongued silence stacked
leaf over leaf
in body, soul
and shadow

> *one cup I've had*
> *of lemon-colored light*
> *then one of lavender*
> *one of night*

I don't know if she flew out to die
as they will, when it's time
or the scent of late summer phlox
and the moon of my reading light
called the honey bee I found
bumping my lampshade
as I read,
vespers gone and compline
slanting blue down the mountain

> *one cup I've had*
> *of lemon-colored light*
> *then one of lavender*
> *one of night*

Carefully I cupped
and carried her into the
cicada-thrumming dark
and shook her into the mint bed

worried about the chill
and hush-winged owls, but
so glad there were stars

> *one cup I've had*
> *of lemon-colored light*
> *then one of lavender*
> *one of night*

Sanctuary

The shining woman digs red clay from the river
then washes, works and shapes a bowl
in the arc length of an ibex horn
and deep flexure of a mare's belly
before she gives birth

This is given to the temple of fire
as a sacrifice and a path

❦

Inside it is glazed with salt and lightwaves
blue-green elf cups on rotting wood
prickling of hope
tiny up-urges burning on the breaking down
and the ocean healing of an accelerating universe

How bluely it presses out
and brings with it wind, fragrant
with a world here, but unimaginably far
passing through

How does life expand?
it swells, ripens
until it is light as a seed
it does

❦

The outside of her breathing bowl
remains porous clay—dirt, really
          —*adamah*, the old rabbis say

absorbing the shadow and trembling waves
that come as a part of love, imperfect as it is

There are debts and laments,
scorch marks the color of a crow's wing
a song now behind, now ahead
of the thorn and vector of our grief

How can this increase love?
night bows before the consequence of day
your beloved's arms encircle you still
they do

❧

You are this shining bowl, beloved
in your robe of fen and flame
in your sanctuary of singing weeds
and drunken fruit

You are the holy of holies
and you will be, and be more
you will

www.ingramcontent.com/pod-product-compliance
Lightning Source LLC
Chambersburg PA
CBHW070915280326
41934CB00008B/1726